Y0-CRD-142

CONTEMPLATION AND COMPASSION
THOMAS MERTON'S VISION

by

A N T H O N Y T. P A D O V A N O

Illustrated by

P a u l a   J.   G o o d m a n

PETER PAUPER PRESS, INC.
White Plains, New York

Peter Pauper Press books are distributed in the United States by Kampmann & Company, Inc., 9 East 40th Street, New York, New York 10016.

ISBN 0-88088-104-6
Library of Congress Catalog Card No. 84-60721

Acknowledgements of permission to use copyrighted material appear on page 63.

Printed in the United States of America
0987654321

Dedication

*For my wife, Theresa, on our tenth
wedding anniversary*

*For my mother, Mary, on her fiftieth
wedding anniversary and on her
graduation from college*

*For Mark Anthony, Andrew Anthony,
Paul Anthony, Rosemarie Theresa*

C O N T E N T S

INTRODUCTION

Thomas Merton was a man of enormous appeal and lasting influence. There is a mystery about him, an elusiveness. He was one of the most arresting personalities of the Twentieth Century.

Thomas Merton was born in France on January 31, 1915 of two artist parents, his father, a New Zealander, his mother, an American. He was from the beginning a person who could not be defined by one nation or group. Later in his life he would be as at home in the Orient as in the West, as comfortable with Buddhism as with Christianity, as much at ease with folk singers as with philosophers, an adviser to civil rights and church leaders, rabbis, poets, and mystics.

Merton grew up in New York City but also attended schools in France and England. Both of his parents died young; his only sibling, a younger brother, was killed in World War II. Merton was, therefore, homeless and without family for most of his life. He felt lost and wan-

9

dered geographically and psychologically to find himself and a place where he truly belonged. He immersed himself in alcohol, in anarchy, in wild behavior, and in promiscuous sex. Nothing settled him; the emptiness remained.

Merton sensed in himself a spiritual longing for a purity and fidelity which eluded his self indulgence. He was attracted to Catholicism. At Columbia University in New York City, he pursued an academic career and, while studying for a doctorate in English literature, was baptized. Soon after, in 1941, he entered the Abbey of Gethsemani, Kentucky when he was twenty-six years of age.

Already present in the life of Merton were many of the elements which would later contribute to his greatness and to his appeal. He was universal in his outlook, secular and bold in his life experience yet somehow sensitive to viable spiritual values. He was educated, articulate, self-preoccupied, seemingly on an endless journey to a destination he could not easily discern. These elements are characteristic of the Twentieth Century. The ability of Merton to absorb these experiences in his own person and to write about them gracefully and vividly led many of his readers to believe that in reading Merton they were encountering themselves.

Merton became a Cistercian monk. Cistercians abstain from meat, rise at two in the morning, remain silent while they are in the monastery, work for hours in the fields, and pray constantly through the day. Merton had once been self indulgent; he seemed now to have gone to another extreme. Yet, the new life of rigor and discipline settled him and released in him a tremendous burst of creative energy. His 27 years as a monk would bring him greatness, sanctity perhaps, happiness most assuredly.

Seven years after Merton entered the Cistercian Abbey of Gethsemani, he published *Seven Storey Mountain* (1948), an autobiographical account of his pilgrimage from chaos to peace. The book struck a sensitive chord throughout the world. It was a best seller in the United States and has been translated widely. His story manifests the possibility of spiritual serenity and personal tranquility in a century of turmoil and unrest.

During Merton's lifetime, he published 60 books and 600 articles and became recognized as a spiritual guide, a contemporary critic, a poet, a mystic, and an activist for social reform. He broke stereotypical molds and eluded the traditional definition of a monk and a contemplative. He became active in civil rights, nuclear disarmament, and protest against the Vietnam war. During this time he became a hermit and continued to lead others by his writings from the hermitage.

Merton's appeal to Twentieth Century men

and women appears to lie in the paradoxes in his life and writings. In this century we have tried to affirm the sacred without abandoning the secular; Merton was deeply involved in monastic life and yet a citizen of the secular world. We have insisted on personal integrity and self-actualization but need authority systems if the human family is to survive; Merton was very much his own person, functioning within a strict monastic order. We see ourselves as open to other cultures; Merton became fascinated with Oriental religions, and learned spiritual and personal wisdom from Western and Eastern religious systems.

Merton was always on a journey. He emerged as the universal person we in the Twentieth Century admire, and he did this in a most startling manner. He was rooted in Catholicism as priest and monk and yet belonged to all religions. He was an American by choice and conviction whose global outlook made those in other nations sense him as one of their own. It was a magnificent personal and professional achievement.

It is this extraordinary man who will be our guide through this book. His life of adventure and risk, of journey and commitment, of human depth and spiritual exaltation gives us an insight into ourselves and into the world and century in which we live.

We begin each page with a quotation from Merton and then reflect on its meaning. The meditation which follows each quotation is not in Merton's words but is rooted in his thought and philosophy. The text remains sensitive to Merton throughout and develops his ideas in a direction he would have approved. The book is meant to serve as an introduction to Merton for those who know little of him and as a refinement of Merton for those who are well versed in his work.

Merton died of accidental electrocution on December 10, 1968 in Bangkok, Thailand while on a journey to the Orient for spiritual and personal meaning. His death, like his life, is a symbol of pilgrimage, a sign of searching, perhaps also an experience of fulfillment. He is buried at the Abbey of Gethsemani. In some way, perhaps, we can sense him still alive in these pages.

O R I G I N S

Self

First Quotation: *God utters me like a word containing a thought of Himself. A word will never be able to comprehend the voice that utters it.*

Seeds of Contemplation

Our words are personal expressions of ourselves. This is why we are grateful when people listen to us. Listening is the way we accept one another as persons. We are offended when people pay no attention to our words. Refusing to hear the words of another may be the most profound form of rejection.

We are God's words. God speaks and creation happens. God is offended whenever we are deaf to one another and blessed whenever we attend to one another.

We are the resonance of God's voice, the echo of God's love. When God calls, we are born struggling, writhing, laboring through our mother's body into existence. Then God becomes a whisper in our heart, a conscience, a quiet reminder of the turbulence which hurled us into being.

A word is never as mighty as the thought which makes it. We realize this as we reject certain words as unsuitable to the thought we had in generating them. The thought of God governs the word which we are.

Words are fragile and enduring all at once. They perish even as they are spoken unless they take birth in the hearing and heart of someone else. Words go out into the world seeking an inn in which to be born, a manger which will shelter them. Words, like people, do not survive unless they are accepted. When they are accepted, they endure.

Second Quotation: . . . *before*
a man can become a saint he
must first of all be a man *in*
all the humanity and fragility
of men's actual condition . . .
Life and Holiness

Merton observes that God cannot be found by those who estrange themselves from the human condition. God is encountered, even before God is recognizable as God, in the love men and women bear one another, in the joy that a child creates, in the splendor of sunrise and the sorrow of sunset. God is refracted through the whole range of human emotions like a rainbow that embraces the earth even as it touches the heavens. God is a passionate lover of the human condition. It is God who keeps us as brothers and sisters. It is God who makes darkness yield before the light and who forever breaks the threatening silence with words of love.

There is no way to heaven which does not go through the earth, no door to eternal life which does not open into human life, no path to infinity which is not circumscribed with limits on all sides. God made us to be unsettled moments in a world made up of time and eternity. We are here and there, now and always, immature and ageless, new born and deathless. We are human.

There almost seems to be a divided alle-

giance in us, a desperate conflict of loyalties, a
need to cling to the earth and a realization that
the earth crumbles as it is clutched. Some would
say we are absurd, that there is no hope for us,
that there is something pathetic and perverse in
this torment that makes us yearn for immortality
even as we perish.

But there is no divided allegiance if the earth
and heaven are parts of the same entirety. There
is no desperate conflict of loyalties if fidelity to
human life is the same as faithfulness to God.

For, this is the great mystery, the most sub-
lime of all the thoughts we know, that God is one
of us and all of us, that there is no God except the
God who made us, that the earth is as much
God's home as is heaven, that the human heart
holds God as surely as does the cosmos, that all
things human lead to God, that nothing ever dies
except that which must and that good things pass
into the keeping of God who first set their course
and called them home only when it was right for
them to come home.

Third Quotation: *For me to be a
saint means to be myself.*
Seeds of Contemplation

For some, sanctity is theatre. Some people seek to be saints not because they love God or

18

people but because they love to be on display. For others, sanctity is equated with the cruel rejection of all that we treasure as human beings.

Merton once quoted St. John Chrysostom to the effect that it is vain to punish oneself, to fast and sleep on the ground, to be sorry for one's sins and to deny oneself pleasure, it is vain to do all this if one is of no use to anybody else.

Sanctity means that we do not try forever to be something we are not. It means that we believe God wants us to be happy. It means that we are grateful for the achievements and the failings, for the things that go right and those that go wrong despite our efforts to the contrary. Sanctity should fit in comfortably with our life. Merton once observed that when the shoe fits, the foot is forgotten.

It is not difficult to be a saint. In any case, sanctity does not mean that we are perfect. It means that we care about being better. Sanctity, properly understood, is free and joyous, spontaneous and warm, gratifying and consoling.

Would God call us to an impossible vocation? Would God want us to be in painful pursuit of a sanctity or life we really never wanted or needed?

Relationship

> **Fourth Quotation:** . . . *a faith
> that is afraid of other people is
> no faith at all. A faith that
> supports itself by condemning
> others is itself condemned by the
> Gospel.*
>
> Faith and Violence

Faith does not emerge from a clenched fist but from open arms. There is no faith in fear. The allies of fear are the enemies of love. This Merton knew late in his life after suffering the violence of condemnation by people both within the Church and in the world at large.

We fear others because we fear ourselves. We fear ourselves when we become frightened by the limitations under which we live. But to be human is to be limited. Limitation implies that we are ignorant of many things, even of things we ought to know. Limitation leads us into temptations which entice us to act against our own well-being. We all dislike the fact that our talent and resources go only so far and that death is never as distant as we would like.

God expects us to be sometimes unknowing and often unwilling, to be lured by passion and to act foolishly, to grow fatigued, and to fear dying.

God is not afraid of the human condition.

When we fear ourselves, we fear others. We fear that they may diminish our life. We need to know that the reverses we suffer from others never impede the basic direction of our lives. We lose not what was meaningful in life but a direction we preferred life to have gone. No one can take from us the attitude toward our life that we wish to have.

Faith happens as the fears are quieted, as the storm abates, as the turbulence is arrested, as the winds cease to buffet and the sea is calmed.

Fifth Quotation: *When we extend our hand to the enemy who is sinking in the abyss, God reaches out for both of us . . .*
Seeds of Destruction

If, as we have been saying, faith does not nurture fear, it must at some point in its development cease being afraid of the enemy. Gandhi observes that the enemy is overcome when one no longer regards the enemy as an enemy. Jesus tells us that we all love our friends but it is love of the enemy which gives love its final, radical expression. When we love even the enemy, there is no one else to fear. We are finally and fully free.

One might dance in vengeance and sinister

delight as the enemy sinks into the abyss. But this does not free us from the enemy. The enemy we bury with joy and defeat in laughter lies forever dormant within us and rises to afflict us. The enemy within devastates us.

Death or defeat are no victory over the enemy. Love alone conquers the enemy with a victory that is decisive and total, complete and human, compassionate and divine.

Faith is filled with stories of men and women who cross the borders of bondage, who go from the land of slavery and enter the privileged country of those who harbor no hatred, of those who forgive so readily that they hardly sense a need to forgive. Faith is filled with stories of Samaritans who lift the Jew from the dust, of fathers who embrace prodigal sons, of crucified prophets who pray that God not hold this sin against them.

God reaches out for both of us as the enemy sinks and we struggle to rescue and save. God reaches out for both of us because God was never the enemy of either of us.

Sixth Quotation: *In the union of man and woman it is no longer words that are symbols of the mystery of God's holiness, but persons.*

The New Man

The promise and peril of human relationships are summed up in marriage. There is no relationship capable of bringing us greater joy or deeper sorrow.

Why is it that Thomas Merton, a celibate monk, finds in marriage a capacity to symbolize God that many married people do not?

This disparity may occur because people think of God as different from us in an aloof and almost forbidding manner. Marriage, however, is such an ordinary, such a human experience. Since many suppose God is not near us or like us they regard marriage as too familiar, as too near us for God to be identified with it. Many do not believe that God can be manifested in love which is physical as well as spiritual, in love which is erotic as well as self-giving.

People are unwilling to speak of God in marital terms because they fear the human is unworthy of God and that they themselves are without merit at least in a religious sense. Eventually, this attitude toward marriage and the human condition leads people to doubt all human relationships as a way to God.

The Bible, however, describes God more often in marital terms than in any other. One can see why this is so. If the world were encircled with the love the bridegroom has for the bride, then life would be a joyous marriage feat and God would be known clearly as the lover God truly is.

God

Seventh Quotation: . . . *God rises up
out of the sea like a treasure in
the waves, and when language
recedes His brightness remains on
the shores of our own being.*
Thoughts in Solitude

There are levels on which the encounter
with God occurs. There is the level of quiet awareness that makes the heart sing while the voice is
silent. This may happen as we behold a sunrise or
discover a rainbow, as we gaze at the stars, or
swim in the sea, as we climb a mountain or touch
a flower. This beauty, not of our own making,
where did it come from? What is its purpose?
Why does it have such an effect on us?

There is the level of human sensitivity to
other persons. Here we sing with our bodies the
melody of human sharing even though our voices
are still. This may happen as a mother holds a
baby, as a man and woman weep in each other's
arms, as a father's hand steadies his son, as friends
embrace or lovers touch finger tips in parting.
This yearning to be part of other human lives,
where is its source? What is its meaning or destiny? Why are people so touching, so life giving?

There is the level of exuberance when we

27

seem to know what we are about, when we call God by name, beg for specific graces, and define God in what seem to be manageable categories.

The quotation suggests another level. It may be that the encounter with God is so exquisitely tender and incapable of expression that language breaks down before it. What does one do when the meaning cannot be held, when the music is so haunting that one must do more than hear it? As language recedes, the reality goes on and gratitude becomes unbearable. The shores of our being become flooded with God and we sense that we belong not only to the shore but to the dark and distant, light and near waters of eternity.

> **Eighth Quotation:** *Until we love God perfectly, everything in the world will be able to hurt us. And the greatest misfortune is to be dead to the pain . . .*
> Seeds of Contemplation

There are many things to sort out in life. It is easy for us to know exactly what something is for if we make it ourselves. We found ourselves already made when we came upon ourselves. It is more difficult to know what something is for when it crosses our path than it is when we ourselves set it on its path.

28

Technology teaches us that we can get hurt by a piece of machinery which is not used as its manufacturer intended. We can get hurt and, often, the machinery is damaged. The machine breaks down as an act of protest against those who misuse it.

But what is our purpose? Why do we weep and laugh, hope and despair, love and deny, write poetry, sing songs, count stars, name planets, arrange flowers, tremble in the darkness, dance in the light, roam the earth, come home to people, reach for God?

The most obvious observation about human beings is that they love to be loved. They also love to love in return. Just as flowers become beautiful as they find the soil and sunlight, human beings are transformed in the atmosphere of love. We were made for love and love made us. But whose love and why?

The flower knows in some way that the sunlight is greater than itself. It rejoices and responds. We sense a love more magnificent than our own and turn toward it.

If we become children again and look at this person who we are as a new thing which has crossed our path, we will learn from our observation that each of us is love in a new form. When we truly understand this about ourselves, nothing can hurt us.

Ninth Quotation: *There are two absences of God. One is an absence that condemns us, the other an absence that sanctifies us.*

No Man Is An Island

Merton experienced early in his own life the absence of God occasioned by his immorality. Later, as a monk, he experienced God's absence as a "dark night of the soul." Although God is absent in both cases, the reality of the absence is radically different.

God is sometimes banished by us because we prefer the isolation. We suppose we are relieved of God's demand and presence, of God's commandments and revelations, of God's authority over our life and judgment of our actions, of God's love for us and involvement in our lives.

We banish God but we are not satisfied because the human is insufficient. The more we possess, the more we sense we are slipping away. The desire to have everything worldly is a sign that we do indeed need everything, that we were made for God and nothing else will substitute. It is tragic to be adrift in a world we do not know what to do with, a world we might own but do not control, a world we forever sense belongs to someone else, a world that resists human efforts to make it purely a human enterprise. How can

30

we possess everything in peace, when we do not possess ourselves? How can we own everything in tranquility when death harbors ever closer, a death that takes from us not one thing or another but all things, a death that will not yield before our demands but summons us on its own terms?

God becomes absent from us at times not because we have closed God out but because God is more than we can hold. God becomes distant at times so that we might freely choose God again. God gives way not because we are selfish but because we do not control divine life and love. Such an absence is another form of reality, an act of grace, an action on God's part that preserves us from the illusion that we own God or that we are more than God. Such absence is presence in another form. When God returns, there seems to be more of God and more of us.

Y E A R N I N G

Journey and Illusion

Tenth Quotation: *My Lord God, I have no idea where I am going. I do not see the road ahead of me. I cannot know for certain where it will end. Nor do I really know myself . . .*
Thoughts in Solitude

We are on a journey because we know that something about our self definition is incomplete. Journey is a way of coping with life, a way of responding to the human condition. God seems to have intended the earth as a place of pilgrimage, a sea, as it were, with no safe havens.

Thomas Merton wrote to his philosopher friend Jacques Maritain that he could not abide situations which tried to remove all peril from his life. Security is sometimes the excuse we give for inertia.

The prayer of Merton which we reflect upon reveals him at a time in his life when he is vulnerable. Merton had lived through seventeen years of monastic discipline and contemplative prayer when he writes about his confusion. If such a man could become insecure, there is little reason to blame ourselves for our perplexity. Ignorance about the next step, regret about our last decision, questions about whether we have been good or generous are not signs that something has gone wrong as much as they are indications that we are in touch with our humanity.

Human life is a venture in hope. But all hope is a risk. If we know the outcome, we do not need hope. Hope is an act of trust in ourselves or others, in life or God. It is an attitude of confidence in the journey we are on and its capacity to lead us in the right direction and bring us home. The road may be more circuitous than we wished. But God is on the way with us so that no one need be lost.

Eleventh Quotation: . . . *one who seeks God without culture and without humanism tends inevitably to promote a religion that is irreligious* . . .

Seeds of Destruction

Religion was always meant to be a gentle experience. It is about love and love is not an essentially harsh reality. Religion emerges from the human heart more immediately than it does from the human head. And there is something compassionate about the heart. This is why we describe the unfeeling as heartless. The journey to faith is a compassionate pilgrimage. The true believers in every generation are those who touch the heart and heal people by the gentle grace of their lives.

Religion becomes cruel in the hands of fanatics, heartless when its language and symbols are used as weapons. It was never meant to be such. The faith religion must nurture is not only faith in God but faith in the goodness of people, faith in the power of truth to prevail, faith in the capacity of people to know what is best for them and to choose rightly.

Religion fails because religion loses its faith, its faith in people, its faith in God to lead people lovingly and gently to the truth, its faith in the rightness of what it is about.

35

When we believe in people, they try to measure up to that trust for the most part, to justify our faith in them, to adjust their behavior so that they do not disappoint those who have placed confidence in them.

God does not desert or disappoint people who keep their faith in human goodness.

Twelfth Quotation: *You never find happiness until you stop looking for it.*
The Way of Chuang Tzu

Happiness, like love, may not always be given to those who work hardest for it. Happiness may be as much a gift as is love. We cannot make people love us. They choose to do this and do this sometimes for the most extraordinary reasons and with the most baffling motives.

There is an element of spontaneity in happiness, something unselfconscious and unplanned. We cannot make others love us if we are too intent upon the enterprise or if we place our hopes for love on the cleverness of the stratagems by which we seek to achieve it. In like manner, happiness is elusive when it is intended directly or pursued with supposedly failure-proof principles for the acquisition of happiness.

Happiness is a process of entering into life

with no specific agenda about what we want from it. A pragmatic culture such as we have in the United States favors goal setting and expects happiness to be one of the goals listed in a life plan. But happiness, like love, is not subject to our control.

We know that love depends as much upon the other in a relationship as it depends upon us. Happiness, likewise, is not entirely of our making. When we cease to pursue happiness for its own sake and enter into life generously, happiness is given to us by life itself. This happiness is given not because we achieved it on our own but because God made it possible for all those who care about the happiness of others.

Justice and Mercy

Thirteenth Quotation: . . . *conflict resolution is one of the crucial areas of theological investigation in our time* . . .

Faith and Violence

We become aware of how important we are by the effect we have on other people. We are crucial to the lives of those who need us to bring them peace. We are, in the biblical allusion, our brother's keeper. We are all lost children, wandering sheep, frightened lovers. Everytime someone brings us peace, everytime we quiet a trembling heart, the sanctity and majesty of God is made manifest, the glory and grace of the human condition is revealed.

The peacemakers become the children of God, as the beattitudes tell us. God is the eye of peace in the hurricane of the cosmos and in the turbulence of our lives. God is the still point of the turning world, the dancer who holds the dance, the melody which sustains the music.

Merton was a man of peace, indeed an apostle of non-violence at a time when this approach had little social support. He preached and practiced conflict resolution; he urged that we bring

39

about peace not only in the world at large but in our own hearts. Thus, each one of us must become the familiar face, the gentle arms, the loving voice, the speaker of God's promises for the infant and the elderly, the weak and the brave, the children and parents of this world.

Peace is the gift and the greeting the Easter Christ offers the troubled disciples. The Easter Christ continues to speak of peace but not now with his own words. He promises peace through every parent who loves a child, to every dying person who finds confidence in someone else's arms, through every husband who assures his wife the marriage was worth a lifetime, to every guilty individual whom another forgives fully and freely.

Fourteenth Quotation: . . . *the anxiety to possess what I should not have narrows and diminishes my own soul.*
No Man Is An Island

Merton spoke often and harshly about the corrupting influence of affluence and technology. He feared that both of these had the capacity to make people insensitive to their own humanity and even to the grace of God.

There is an addiction to affluence at the core

40

of American culture, an addiction which makes us desperate for wealth because wealth is equated with worth. This leads many to attend to the other in terms of that person's money.

Merton observed that equating wealth and happiness is an illusion. The wealthy in reality are, for the most part, not happy but bored. This is especially true if the acquisition of wealth has been a life goal. Wealth gives us too much control over life. At the same time, it creates a pernicious insecurity because one's worth as a person can be taken away by another if that worth is tied up with possessions. If one's worth is in oneself, no thief can steal it.

The boredom and insecurity wealth generates are complicated by the aloofness wealth forces on the rich. One is never sure if the other cares about oneself because of the money one possesses or because the person is valued in his or her own right. Indeed, the wealthy come to distrust their own children. Wealth is far more confining than many of the non-wealthy realize.

Gratitude for what we have is the essence of creative frugality and of happiness. If we are happy, we require less. One need not desperately collect money, houses, friends, or fame if one is grateful.

The only reality we can divide and multiply at the same time is love. Love is increased when it is shared. Wealth and power, fame and possessions are diminished when they are shared. They make us, therefore, regard others as competitors rather than as partners.

> **Fifteenth Quotation:** *Only the admission of defect and fallibility in oneself makes it possible for one to become merciful to others.*
> Gandhi on Non-Violence

There is something in the human soul which requires exuberance and magnificence, magnanimity and generosity. Merton came to realize this when, as he tells us in *Seven Storey Mountain,* he wanted to give himself wholly to God and to experience from God and others forgiveness for his own excesses. Love and forgiveness exceed all bounds. Love is best when the cost is not counted, when one loves even unto death, when the other is loved not because the love has been earned but because the other is who he or she is.

Forgiveness is most effective when it is granted even if the other has not atoned. It is best when it is not given in proportion to the degree of repentance but exceeds it. Forgiveness is most generous when we forgive because the other needs this to go on with life. Forgiveness is most impressive when it is present before the other sought it. One merely forgets the injury and remembers

42

all that is good about the other.

It is magnanimity which moves the human heart and makes the world hopeful about its future.

Mercy is the step beyond justice we are obliged to take so that the world might be governed not by equity but by human compassion and divine grace.

We are all fallible and we have all fallen. It is not the task of mercy to count the sins and punish the offender. Mercy picks the woman from the dust and defends her. Mercy enfolds the son who weeps in our arms after his prodigal ways. Mercy forgives us for the complex drives which make us harm people because we do not know what else to do for our happiness.

It is not a judge or a court of law which saves the world. It is a merciful father and a forgiving mother. The human race cannot become a family by each having his or her rights protected or injuries redressed. Justice allows survival. It assures the minimal behavior we require if human life is to continue. And this is good. But human beings need more than survival if they are to survive.

Mercy recognizes that all of us are sinners and that unless we are all forgiven more than we deserve there is no hope for any of us. Justice is concerned with our rights but mercy is involved with our life.

43

Anxiety and Hope

Sixteenth Quotation: . . . *you must help . . . people simply for the love of it . . . Don't demand appreciation . . . Appreciate* them.

Seeds of Destruction

There is a remarkable saying in Chinese Taoism which observes that a leader has done his work perfectly when he causes those he has led to suppose they never needed him at all.

Even though most of us are not capable of perfect love, it is important that we know such love exists. We may not be capable of loving in so selfless a manner that the response we look for in the other is not gratitude but the other's happiness.

Merton does not ask that we reach the ideal we refer to in Chinese Taoism. He does note, however, that our terrible need to be appreciated is sometimes more crucial to us than the people we are supposedly helping. There is a hint in this of manipulation on our part. We try to keep the other in a subservient position, hesitant to deal with him or her as an equal. On the surface, we seem to be more benign than we are.

We do not wish to discourage people who

are trying to help others by insisting upon so impossible an ideal that they lose heart. But we must be attentive to the risk as well as the privilege in helping others. One day, their lives must go on without us and we ought to rejoice in this.

<blockquote>
Seventeenth Quotation: *The hope that rests on calculation has lost its innocence.*

Raids on the Unspeakable
</blockquote>

Children are naturally hopeful. This may have something to do with their sensitivity to the marvel of life. They do not calculate or plan. They prefer to be surprised.

There are some realities in life whose value can be judged by the effect they have on us. People may argue persuasively that there is no reason for hope. To an extent, they are correct. Hope has no reasons. The value of hope may be demonstrated by what it does to us. It makes us creative; it nourishes love; it enables us to free ourselves from the paralysis of our problems. Despair, on the other hand, does not create; it destroys. There is no reason for hope except the fact that life requires its presence.

No one planned his or her life. One simply came to be. If the coming into existence has such meaning, one can assume that the going forth

carries that meaning with it. If birth causes people to be hopeful, one can affirm that there is hope in life itself.

That which most of us term tragedy may not be tragedy in the largest sense of that term. It may mean nothing more than the failure of our plans. But the universe does not work according to a human plan. The reverses we suffer may be another form of life rather than the end of the road.

In spite of all the odds ranged against it, life endures and develops. For reasons no one knows, the world never exhausts the energy of life and of love but constantly renews it. Most of us realize this at some level of consciousness. Therefore, we sleep in peace and dream bravely, sing in the darkness and dance at dawn.

Eighteenth Quotation: *The proud man claims honor for having what no one else has. The humble man begs for a share in what everybody else has received.*
Thoughts in Solitude

The isolation and loneliness many of us feel is the result of living with illusions. We suppose we are different from people and try to make ourselves different by the roles we play in life. When we act in this manner, we struggle against others and compete. We assume that winning is everything and that people are often obstacles.

When we get beyond what Merton called the shadow and the disguise, we learn that we are not alone and that in defeating other people we defeat ourselves. With this insight Merton hoped to liberate us from the compulsions and neurotic fears which diminish our life.

The proud person wishes to be like no one else, not, of course, to be isolated but to be noticed and, best of all, to be envied. There is a paradox in this attitude. The proud person desires and dislikes people at the same time. He or she wants people as an audience but keeps people at a distance when human bonding enters the process. Praise from others is sought but no commitments are given. The proud person knows that he or she lives in an illusionary world. If people get too close, they will see that the proud person is not as wonderful as he or she pretends to be.

The humble person rejoices in the ecstasy of the ordinary. The humble person feels privileged and graced merely to have been included in life. He or she has learned the great lesson about the one-ness we all share. The humble person is free to enter into life as he or she is. Nothing troubles a proud person more than meeting someone who is liberated from the illusions of pride.

48

D E S T I N Y

Prayer and Contemplation

Nineteenth Quotation: *If you have never had any distractions you don't know how to pray.*
Seeds of Contemplation

We often suppose that prayer is meant to be a perfect experience. People may be reluctant to pray because they feel they are not worthy or because they fear they cannot communicate with God in a meaningful manner. They begin to pray and find their mind is flooded with trivia and distractions. They assume they do not know how to pray and so they cease praying or they pray with half a heart and are constantly disappointed.

Thomas Merton devoted his life to learning how to pray well. He came to understand that perfection in prayer is not only impossible but also undesirable. The quest for perfection in prayer could make people so goal oriented and so conscious of their own achievement that God would be neglected in the process.

The less we know about something the more rigid we tend to be. The less we know the more unreal and exaggerated our expectations may be. When we know little about prayer, we believe that prayer ought to be eloquent and distraction-free. We feel the prayer is inadequate if it does not lead to ecstasy.

But prayer is meant to be as ordinary as reflecting on ourselves or others, as simple as the conversations we have with people we love. We cannot reflect without distraction even though we care a lot about the people we hold in our thoughts. It is no wonder, then, that we are distracted when we reflect on God or converse with God. This does not mean that we do not care about God nor does it mean the prayer has failed. All it means is that we are human.

Twentieth Quotation: *A contemplative is not one who takes his prayer seriously, but one who takes God seriously, who is famished for truth, who seeks to live in generous simplicity ...*
Spiritual Direction and Meditation

Sometimes the most obvious realities are not as apparent as they ought to be. The gift a contemplative may give us is an awareness that we are not to overlook that which is before our eyes. It becomes clear that God is more important than prayer only when it is pointed out to us.

Prayer is a technique, a means for reaching God. People do not communicate effectively by paying careful attention to the words they speak. Indeed, it might be argued that we are anxious about every word we say when we are dealing with people who make us feel insecure. It is the presence people experience when they are together which is always more crucial than the words they share. This does not mean that words do not matter but that something else matters more.

Since God is more important than prayer, God reaches us even when we do not pray, even if we never pray. If we care about life and handle people reverently, we encounter God although we may not be aware of this. There are wordless ways, silent ways, for the human heart to dis-

52

cover and hold on to God.

When we formulate prayer or verbal communication with God, the bonding deepens. People who love each other cherish the words they share even as they know that the presence of the beloved is the point of all their affection. It is not prayer which brings us God. God is there already. Prayer is merely the recognition and joy we feel when we realize God is nearby.

> **Twenty-First Quotation:** [*Contemplation*] *is a country whose center is everywhere and whose circumference is nowhere. You do not find it by travelling but by standing still.*
>
> Seeds of Contemplation

The quotation is arresting, the meaning more elusive at first sight than it is in reflection. Merton reminds us of a truth he repeated in his writings: contemplation is not exotic but something we are all meant to experience.

Contemplation is the sense of one-ness we feel with life as such, with the universe, with other people, with God. There are moments when we experience this peace and harmony. Such moments are the most wonderful moments of life. They are also the substance of contemplation although people do not readily know this.

Contemplation does not occur because people go to a special place, a monastery, for example, or a hermitage. It does not come about merely because people try to bring it about by rigid discipline, self-conscious asceticism, or perfect techniques. Contemplation occurs because we live fully and deeply. It abides beneath the surface of life. It is the gift or grace we are granted when we seek more than empty, transient, self-indulgent experiences.

One need not travel but merely stand still and one is in a contemplative environment. Contemplation can occur in a kitchen or an office, in a bedroom or a board room, on a walk or on a jet, shopping for groceries or wandering in the woods. We are encircled with love and with peace and with God. When we become aware of this, we become one with it. From such experiences we derive courage and joy, exuberance and silence, grace and hope.

Mystery and Silence

Twenty-Second Quotation: ... *it is not he who has many possessions that is rich, but he who has no needs.*
Raids on the Unspeakable

People in an affluent society have a tendency to feel deprived constantly. No matter how much one possesses one always seems to be in need when affluence is the object of one's endeavors. Many people possess more than they can use. They possess things they can find no reason for having except that the having of them seems important. Affluent societies create the illusion that meaning, and even immortality, is possible if one has sufficient material resources.

One is not rich, in human terms, because one reaches a certain economic bracket. One is humanly rich when one is satisfied with that which one has. Indeed, the fullest satisfaction comes about when we come to terms with the realities we were given freely at birth and with those that are available to us at no cost. We are wealthy when we nurture the human emotions and human relationships which keep us in close contact with our humanity.

Affluence, however, creates distance from

the very human-ness which is the essence of our happiness. Children associate easily with one another across barriers of affluence, race, or religion which adults often find difficult to bridge. They do this because they seek in other children a sense of their common childhood or humanity.

When we realize that we have all we need, when we are no longer dominated by acquisitiveness and greed, when we are grateful for what we are worth in non-economic terms, then we become peaceful and rich indeed.

Twenty-Third Quotation: *It is not speaking that breaks our silence, but the anxiety to be heard.*
Thoughts in Solitude

We are familiar with the silence of hostility. Sometimes people do not speak but the wordless rage is worse. We are also acquainted with the silence which seeks attention. In this case, the person is so intent on being noticed that he or she seeks to be different. In these instances, we are dealing with taciturnity rather than silence. True silence is loving and communicative. Speaking does not shatter but complements this silence.

Silence, as Merton envisions it, is linked with tranquility. The silence Merton refers to is the silence which finds place for the other. It is a silence which listens to the other rather than excluding or rejecting him or her.

The point of silence in human development is not economy of words or absence of speech. The silence which humanizes us is the silence emerging from reverence for life and for others. To listen, one must be humble and sensitive, willing to allow the other to speak, truly interested in what the other has to say. It is not monologue but dialogue which creates life.

As we grow to human maturity and care for the life of others, we become creatively and beautifully silent. We evoke words from the other and generate life by our listening. The silent person invites the other into the world and makes that person feel valuable. The silent person is not the one who never speaks but the one who knows how to listen well. When such a person does speak, it is clear to the other that he or she has finally been heard.

> **Twenty-Fourth Quotation:** *The life of every man is a mystery of solitude and communion. ...*
> The Living Bread

We have journeyed a long way in these pages with Thomas Merton as our spiritual mentor. We have reflected on our origins and our yearning, on our destiny and meaning. We begin in a mystery no one can comprehend. We pass into a mystery that no one of us understands. Human life is enveloped in mystery from birth to death. Merton's thought and life experience have helped us realize the depth and creative potential involved in this mystery.

We began with one of Merton's most arresting thoughts: God utters us as a word which is incapable of grasping the voice which generates it. This element of dealing with more than we can clarify is alluded to again in this final reference. We are a mystery of solitude and communion.

The solitude fosters self development and enables us to discover our uniqueness as persons. This solitude requires that we withdraw from others at times, not because they are unworthy but because we are incomplete. Such solitude is the basis for prayer and contemplation, for wonder before mystery and silence itself.

But silence is related to speaking. We are made not only for self definition but for self donation, for coherence with ourselves and communion with others. And so the human equation is imbalanced until others become a factor in our life.

God is a mystery of solitude and communion and we are made in God's image. It is God who is silent and speaks a Word, who is alone

and also a Trinity, who is self-sufficient and yet self-giving in creation.

We have developed this series of meditations in the hope that we have learned solitude from them. But the purpose of the solitude is a deeper communion as we reach out of the silence for the words which tell others and God how much we love.

THE AUTHOR

Anthony Thomas Padovano has doctorates in theology (Rome, Italy) and literature (New York City) as well as a graduate degree in philosophy. He has full professorships in English literature and in Catholic theology.

Dr. Padovano has published thirteen books. He is the author of the recently published *The Human Journey* (Doubleday), a study of Thomas Merton.

Dr. Padovano has lectured around the world and served as summer visiting professor at twenty American colleges and universities. He is listed in *Who's Who in the World, Who's Who in America,* and *Who's Who in Religion.*

PERMISSIONS